DISCOVER DOGS WITH THE AMERICAN CANINE ASSOCIATION

I LIKE BASSET HOUNDS!

Linda Bozzo

It is the mission of the American Canine Association (ACA) to provide registered dog owners with the educational support needed for raising, training, showing, and breeding the healthiest pets expected by responsible pet owners throughout the world. Through our activities and services, we encourage and support the dog world in order to promote best-known husbandry standards as well as to ensure that the voice and needs of our customers are quickly and properly addressed.

Our continued support, commitment, and direction are guided by our customers, including veterinary, legal, and legislative advisors. ACA aims to provide the most efficient, cooperative, and courteous service to our customers and strives to set the standard for education and problem solving for all who depend on our services.

For more information, please visit www.acacanines.com, email customerservice@acadogs.com, phone 1-800-651-8332, or write to the American Canine Association at PO Box 121107, Clermont, FL 34712.

Published in 2018 by Enslow Publishing, LLC.
101 W. 23rd Street, Suite 240, New York, NY 10011

Library of Congress Cataloging-in-Publication Data

Names: Bozzo, Linda, author.
Title: I like basset hounds! / Linda Bozzo.
Description: New York, NY : Enslow Publishing, 2018. | Series: Discover dogs with the american canine association | Audience: Grades K-3. | Includes bibliographical references and index.
Identifiers: LCCN 2017009486| ISBN 9780766091276 (paperback) | ISBN 9780766091283 (6 pack) | ISBN 9780766091290 (library bound)
Subjects: LCSH: Basset hound—Juvenile literature.
Classification: LCC SF429.B2 B69 2018 | DDC 636.753/6—dc23
LC record available at https://lccn.loc.gov/2017009486

Printed in China

To Our Readers: We have done our best to make sure all websites in this book were active and appropriate when we went to press. However, the author and the publisher have no control over and assume no liability for the material available on those websites or on any websites they may link to. Any comments or suggestions can be sent by email to customerservice@enslow.com.

Photo Credits: Cover, p. 1 Anna Mandrikyan/Shutterstock.com; p. 3 (left) Jne Valokuvaus/Shutterstock.com; pp. 3 (right), 9 Dr. Alan Lipkin/Shutterstock.com; p. 5 DLILLC/Corbis/VCG/Getty Images; p. 6 Ewais/Shutterstock.com; p. 10 Ksenia Raykova/Shutterstock.com; p. 13 (puppy) Ermolaev Alexander/Shutterstock.com; p. 13 (collar) graphicphoto/iStock/Thinkstock, (bed) Luisa Leal Photography/Shutterstock.com, (brush) In-Finity/Shutterstock.com, (food and water bowls) exopixel/Shutterstock.com, (leash, toys) © iStockphoto.com/Liliboas; pp. 14, 21 RosetteJordaan/E+/Getty Images; p. 17 Sidra Monreal Photography/Shutterstock.com; p. 18 Jupiterimages/Stockbyte/Thinkstock; p. 19 Gabriela Tulian/Shutterstock.com.

Enslow Publishing
101 W. 23rd Street
Suite 240
New York, NY 10011
USA
enslow.com

CONTENTS

IS A BASSET HOUND RIGHT FOR YOU?

Basset hounds are great family dogs. They are gentle with children. If you have other pets, a basset hound might be right for you.

Basset hounds were bred to be hunting dogs. They pick up scents from animals such as rabbits.

A DOG OR A PUPPY?

Basset hound puppies can be slow to train. If you do not have time to train a puppy, you may want an older basset hound instead.

Basset hounds, though medium in height, have large, heavy bodies.

LOVING YOUR BASSET HOUND

Love your basset hound by letting him try to fit in your lap. He will like to be snuggled up close to you.

Basset hounds are happy to lie in a warm, sunny spot indoors.

EXERCISE

Basset hounds need regular walks on a **leash** to stay fit. This breed is not very playful, but games like **fetch** will keep your basset hound from gaining weight.

Being overweight can cause basset hounds to have back problems.

FEEDING YOUR BASSET HOUND

Basset hounds love to eat! They can be fed wet or dry dog food. Ask a **veterinarian (vet)**, a doctor for animals, which food is best for your dog and how much to feed her.

Give your basset hound fresh, clean water every day.

Remember to keep your dog's food and water dishes clean. Dirty dishes can make a dog sick.

Do not feed your dog people food. It can make her sick.

Your new dog will need:

a collar with a tag

a bed

a brush

food and water dishes

a leash

toys

A basset hound's droopy lower eyelids and long ears need to be cleaned often.

GROOMING

Basset hounds **shed** all year around. This means their hair falls out. Brushing your basset hound weekly will help to keep his coat clean and shiny.

Basset hounds have short legs so they are close to the ground. They get dirty very easily and will need to be bathed. Use a gentle soap made just for dogs. A basset hound's nails will need to be clipped. A vet or **groomer** can show you how. Your dog's ears should be cleaned, and his teeth should be brushed by an adult.

WHAT YOU SHOULD KNOW

Basset hounds are calm and a bit lazy. They drool a lot! If left alone for long periods of time, they can howl loudly. Basset hounds are not good swimmers.

You will need to take your new dog to the vet for a checkup. He will need shots, called vaccinations, and yearly checkups to keep him healthy. If you think your dog may be sick or hurt, call your vet.

A GOOD FRIEND

The basset hound you bring into your home will be your best friend. She will enjoy being a member of your family for a long time.

Basset hounds can live as long as 10 to 12 years.

NOTE TO PARENTS

It is important to consider having your dog spayed or neutered when the dog is young. Spaying and neutering are operations that prevent unwanted puppies and can help improve the overall health of your dog.

It is also a good idea to microchip your dog, in case he or she gets lost. A vet will implant a microchip under the skin containing an identification number that can be scanned at a vet's office or animal shelter. The microchip registry is contacted, and the company uses the ID number to look up your information from a database.

Some towns require licenses for dogs, so be sure to check with your town clerk.

For more information, speak with a vet.

There are many dogs, young and old, waiting to be adopted from animal shelters and rescue groups.

Words to Know

fetch To go after a toy and bring it back.

groomer A person who bathes and brushes dogs.

leash A chain or strap that attaches to the dog's collar.

shed When dog hair falls out so new hair can grow.

vaccinations Shots that dogs need to stay healthy.

veterinarian (vet) A doctor for animals.

Read About Dogs

Books

Callen, Sharon. *Boris the Basset.* Huntington Beach, CA: Teacher Created Materials, 2014.

Carney, Elizabeth. *Woof! 100 Fun Facts About Dogs.* Washington, DC: National Geographic Children's Books, 2017.

Gray, Susan H. *Basset Hounds.* New York, NY: AV2 by Weigl, 2016.

Websites

American Canine Association Inc., Kids Corner
www.acakids.com

Visit the official website of the American Canine Association.

National Geographic for Kids, Pet Central
kids.nationalgeographic.com/explore/pet-central

Learn more about dogs and other pets at the official site of the National Geographic Society for Kids.

INDEX